CIRCUS OF FEARS

T0020164

ROAR!

Nasty NATURE PHOBIAS

by John Wood &
Noah Leatherland

BEARPORT
PUBLISHING

Minneapolis, Minnesota

Credits

Images are courtesy of Shutterstock.com. With thanks to Getty Images, Thinkstock Photo, and iStockphoto. RECURRING – pikepicture, kantimar kongjaidee, MagicMary. COVER – Sochillplanets, dhtgip, Kozlovskiy Andrey, Toma Stepunina, Macrovector, Denys Koltovskyi, OP38Studio, KLUSER. 4–5 – sicegame, Tom Wang, Mad Dog. 6–7 – andrejs polivanovs, Aastels, Inspiring. 8–9 – nutsiam, unjiko, EsHanPhot, Anton-Burakov, Dzm1try, Ammak. 10–11 – Darlene Wagner Butler, Pongsak14, dgultig, Butterfly Hunter. 12–13 – Macrovector, gie23, Vasin Lee. 14–15 – Diwas Designs, Yannick Morelli, M-SUR, Ludovic Farine, Mima40. 16–17 – altafulla, Lukasz Pawel Szczepanski, AJR_photo, Vectorpic, PodiumStore. 18–19 – Pimonpim T, Toma Stepunina, SuslO. 20–21 – Photo Spirit, Denis Andricic, Platoo Studio. 22–23 – natrot, r.kathesi, Elena Chevalier, Amado Designs, Anne Czichos. 24–25 – Vadim Sadovski, nami chwang, mapman, PrintablesPlazza, Tomacco. 26–27 – farzand01, maxbelchenko, VikiVector. 28–29 – superjoseph, Nicolas-SB.

Bearport Publishing Company Product Development Team

President: Jen Jenson; Director of Product Development: Spencer Brinker; Managing Editor: Allison Juda; Associate Editor: Naomi Reich; Associate Editor: Tiana Tran; Art Director: Colin O'Dea; Designer: Elena Klinkner; Designer: Kayla Eggert; Product Development Assistant: Owen Hamlin

Library of Congress Cataloging-in-Publication Data is available at www.loc.gov or upon request from the publisher.

ISBN: 979-8-88916-611-5 (hardcover)
ISBN: 979-8-88916-616-0 (paperback)
ISBN: 979-8-88916-620-7 (ebook)

For more information, write to Bearport Publishing, 5357 Penn Avenue South, Minneapolis, MN 55419.

CONTENTS

WELCOME
★ TO THE ★
SHOW!

COME ONE, COME ALL! SEE THE AMAZING CIRCUS OF FEARS!

Everyone is afraid of something. But do you have a phobia? This is a very strong fear. You may even have a phobia of something that cannot cause you any real danger.

People have phobias of all sorts of things. Some common phobias are of spiders and flying on planes.

Our circus is all about real fears. Are you ready to find out what scares people the most?

Maybe you will leave the show with a brand-new phobia of your own. . . . .

THE SCIENCE OF ★ ★ FEAR

Some scientists think phobias may be passed down by evolution. Evolution is a process in which people and animals change and **adapt** over time.

Long ago, giraffes had short necks. Many scientists believe giraffes' necks evolved to reach leaves in tall trees. This helps them find food other animals cannot reach.

Evolution helps plants, people, and other animals survive. Some of the phobias we have today may have been helpful in the past.

When it's dark, it's difficult for people to see what's around them. In the past, people may have been scared after the sun went down. To avoid danger, they would find somewhere safe to stay at night.

WORRYING WAVES

Waves are some of the most powerful forces in nature. It is no wonder people are afraid of them.

Over time, waves can reshape how the world looks. They wear down the rocks and cliffs on the shore.

During a storm, waves can cause a lot of damage very quickly. They can tip over boats or **destroy** buildings near the coast.

Scientists have recorded waves more than 100 feet (30 m) high. That is about as high as six giraffes standing on top of one another. Watch out for wild water!

PLANT PERIL

What grows in the ground, up walls, and deep in the dirt? Plants! They might move more slowly than you can see, but plants fill some people with terror.

People who are scared of plants may think of them as dangerous. They will do everything they can to avoid them, including staying indoors.

There are some plants that eat bugs alive. Others have deadly poison that can kill anything that eats them.

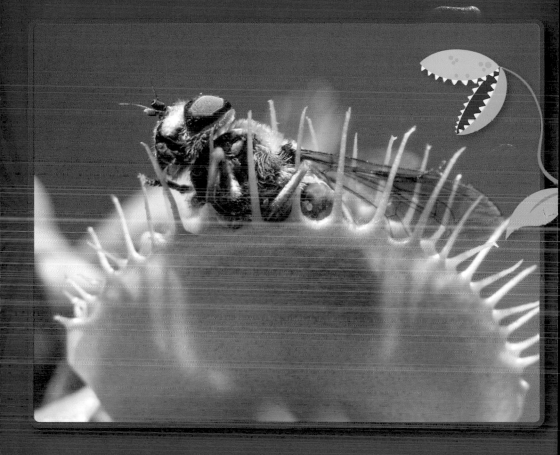

Plants might not be able to chase us, but they can still hurt. Some have **prickly** thorns or stinging nettles. One touch can cause a lot of pain!

HOLES
★ OF ★
HORROR

Clusters of tiny holes could make anybody squirm. They are deep and dark. What could be at the bottom of them?

Some holes are caused by a **disease** taking over the body. Others are made by bugs munching away at a meal.

Many clusters of holes are found in the wild.
Some kinds of rocks have lots of holes in them.
There are plants with holes to hold their seeds.

For some people, a fear
of small holes pops up
because the holes remind
them of something else.
Maybe they feel this way
because some **venomous**
snakes have a pattern of
small holes on their skin.

THUNDER FEAR

Black and gray clouds appear in the sky. Then, rain starts to pour. It's a storm!

For some people, there is nothing scarier. They may shiver at a flash of light in a dark cloud. Some are afraid of the loud clap of thunder.

The fear of thunder and lightning is one of the most common phobias among young people. Many are scared of being struck by lightning.

Animals are often afraid of thunder and lightning, too. Cats and dogs might try to hide during storms.

★ DINGY ★ DARKNESS

Many people are terrified of being in a pitch-black room. How do you feel about the dark?

People with a fear of the dark might be scared about what they can't see. Could there be something else in the room?

A lot of people have a fear of the dark when they are young. Some adults are scared of the dark, too.

Some people have a hard time sleeping in complete darkness. They might use a night-light to help them feel safe while they snooze.

★ LIGHT ★ FRIGHT

Plenty of people are afraid of the dark, but what about the opposite? For some, the light can be just as frightening.

Even though the sun is far away, its light can still reach Earth. It is strong enough to heat up our whole planet.

Some people worry about how the sun will affect their bodies. They are scared of getting sunburned or becoming sick from the sun.

During the day, people who are scared of the light might cover themselves up as much as they can. Others will stay inside until it is dark.

Everyone and everything is being followed. Sometimes these dark and mysterious shapes are small. Other times they are big. What could they be? They are shadows!

No matter what we do, shadows are impossible to escape. Where there is light, there are shadows.

People with a fear of shadows are afraid of the way they stretch and change. The shapes can seem like creepy monsters in the dark.

Others are scared of the way shadows move across walls and floors. The shapes can seem to be alive.

BIG AND SCARY

Some people fear big things, especially if they are more than twice our size! There is a very obvious threat when things loom large.

Sometimes, Jupiter has giant storms that are bigger than the size of Earth. If Jupiter were to switch places with the moon, these storms would be too big to escape from.

From skyscrapers to trains, there are large objects everywhere. For people with this phobia, anything that makes them feel small can be frightening.

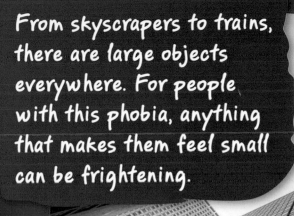

The best way to overcome the fear of big things is to face them little by little. Start by looking at something common, such as a car or bus. Then, slowly move onto looking at larger things until fear stops taking over.

clean-energy bus

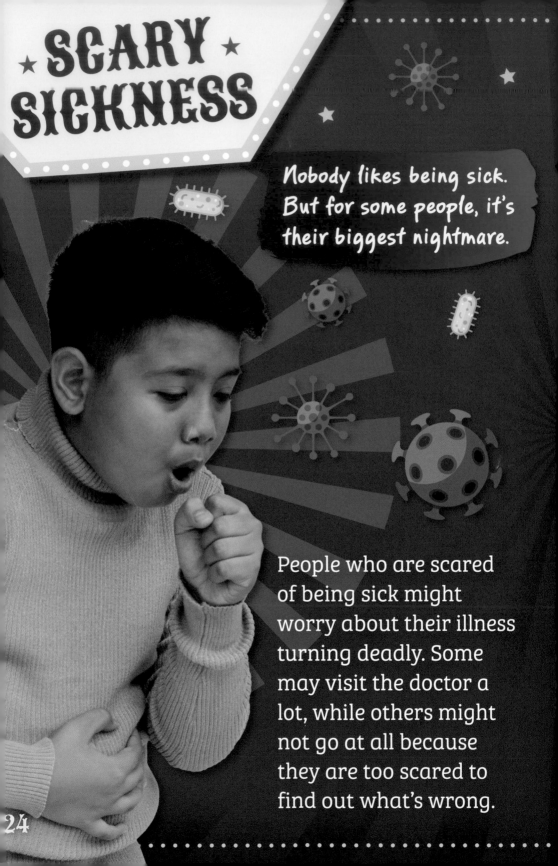

★ SCARY ★ SICKNESS

Nobody likes being sick. But for some people, it's their biggest nightmare.

People who are scared of being sick might worry about their illness turning deadly. Some may visit the doctor a lot, while others might not go at all because they are too scared to find out what's wrong.

The fear of getting sick might make someone act strangely. They may clean or cover themselves up as much as they can. Some people might not even leave their homes!

This phobia is more common in people who study diseases. Maybe it's because they think about illnesses a lot.

CREEPING
★ IN THE ★
DEEP

There is so much of Earth's oceans we have yet to explore. That's because they are so large and deep. And the deeper we go, the darker it gets.

People with a fear of deep water might worry about what lies below the waves. Are there creatures with sharp teeth, long **tentacles**, and slippery **scales** waiting for us?

Sunlight can reach only so far below the water's surface. Everything below 3,000 ft (1,000 m) deep is completely dark. What could be hidden down there?

Over three million ships have sunk to the bottom of the ocean. Because the sea is so deep, these ships are hard to find. Most of them are never seen again.

More than 2,000 years ago, Augustus was the **emperor** of Rome. He ruled over all the land and people that the Romans had taken control of.

Although Augustus was a very smart and powerful leader, he had his own fears.

Augustus was scared of lightning.

He once saw someone struck by lightning. The emperor thought it was a sign the gods were upset. So, he built a **temple** for them. Augustus thought this would make the gods happy and keep him safe.

THANKS FOR COMING! WE HOPE YOU'VE ENJOYED EXPLORING NATURE PHOBIAS. COME BACK SOON!

Stay brave for the next time you are forced to face your fears!

GLOSSARY

adapt to change to work better in a place or situation

clusters groups of things close together

destroy to get rid of completely

disease a sickness or illness

emperor the ruler of a large area of land called an empire

prickly having small, sharp points

scales small, thin plate-like parts that cover the bodies of some animals

temple a building where people go to pray or worship

tentacles long, thin body parts on some animals that are used to feel or hold things

venomous full of poison that can be injected by a bite or sting

INDEX

Read More

Colich, Abby. *Your Brain When You're Scared (Brainpower).* Minneapolis: Jump!, Inc., 2023.

Spalding, Maddie. *Understanding Phobias (Mental Health Guides).* San Diego: BrightPoint Press, 2022.

Learn More Online

1. Go to **www.factsurfer.com** or scan the QR code below.

2. Enter "**Nature Phobias**" into the search box.

3. Click on the cover of this book to see a list of websites.